inspirational journal

with you in mind

Personal Words for My Grandchild

Bonnie Sparrman

KPT PUBLISHING.COM

CONTENTS

"When a child is born,

so are

grandparents."

Most of us feel sure we love our children with every ounce of our being. We live with that understanding until one day it is eclipsed by the arrival of a grandchild! That's when we're shocked to discover the love we had for our children wasn't as complete as we thought. Suddenly this newborn child-of-our-child unlocks an unknown part of our heart that is bursting with an even greater love. We thought we loved our children with our whole heart...but now we've discovered a new love, bigger than any previously known.

It's out of that love for grandchildren that we share our life story. Our memories of seasons and years gone by are a treasure for grandchildren and great-grandchildren for generations to come. Our family legacy is a gift, and there's no better way for our offspring to know their family history than through the words of a loving grandparent.

As you write on these pages, know that you are blessing your family with the goodness God has given you. May you find pleasure in recording your thoughts, ideas, memories, and lessons learned. Don't worry if you need to leave some sections blank. That is to be expected. Just keep in mind that the valuable words you share are a beautiful, lasting gift of love for your family.

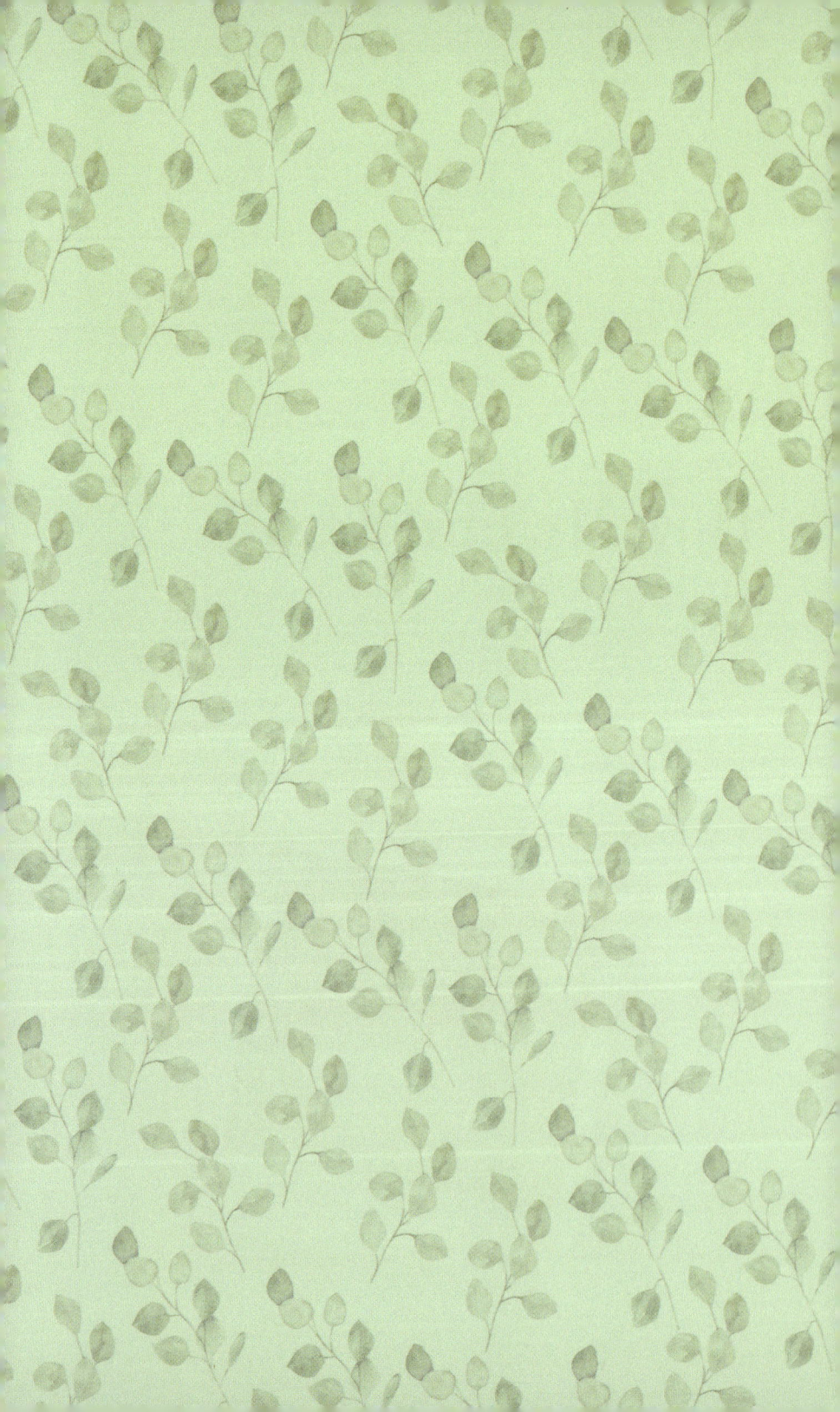

How My Life Began

"*Grandparents,
like heroes,
are as necessary
to a child's growth
as vitamins.*"

Joyce Allston

I was born on: _____
(Date of your birth.) _____

I was born in: _____
(Your birthplace.) _____

My full given name is: _____
_____

I was given this name because: _____
_____
_____
_____
_____

My nickname is: _____
I acquired it... _____
_____
_____
_____
_____

My mother's full name:_____

(Her birthdate and birthplace.)_____

My father's full name: _____

(His birthdate and birthplace.) _____

The names of my siblings: _____

(Their birthdates and birthplaces.) _____

_____

_____

_____

_____

_____

_____

My maternal grandparents: _____

_____

(Their birthdates and birthplaces.)_____

_____

_____

My paternal grandparents: _____

_____

(Their birthdates and birthplaces.) _____

_____

_____

My spouse's full given name: _____

(Birthdate and birthplace.) _____

_____

_____

Our wedding date & place: _____

_____

_____

_____

The names of my children:_____

(Birthdates and birthplaces.) _____

_____

_____

_____

_____

_____

_____

The names of my grandchildren:_____

(Birthdates and birthplaces.) _____

_____

_____

_____

_____

_____

_____

_____

_____

ATTACH PHOTO
WITH
FAMILY MEMBERS

A Few of My Favorite Things

*"Raindrops on roses
and whiskers on kittens,
bright copper kettles and warm woolen mittens,
brown paper packages tied up with strings,
these are a few of my favorite things..."*

OSCAR HAMMERSTEIN

My favorite color is: _____

I like it because... _____

_____

_____

_____

My favorite flower: _____

It reminds me of... _____

_____

_____

_____

My favorite place to take a walk: _____

_____

_____

_____

_____

_____

My favorite book: _____

_____

_____

_____

My favorite author: _____

_____

_____

_____

My favorite Bible verse: _____

_____

_____

_____

_____

_____

_____

_____

My favorite flavor of ice cream: _____

_____

_____

_____

My favorite song: _____

_____

I like it because... _____

_____

_____

_____

My favorite artist: _____

_____

_____

_____

My favorite movie: _____

_____

_____

_____

_____

My favorite sport:_____

_____

_____

_____

_____

My favorite sports team:_____

_____

_____

_____

_____

My favorite leisure activity:_____

_____

_____

_____

_____

_____

_____

_____

_____

PHOTO

PHOTO

My favorite vacation destination: _____

_____

_____

_____

_____

_____

_____

Other favorites I want you to know about: _____

_____

_____

_____

_____

_____

_____

_____

_____

_____

_____

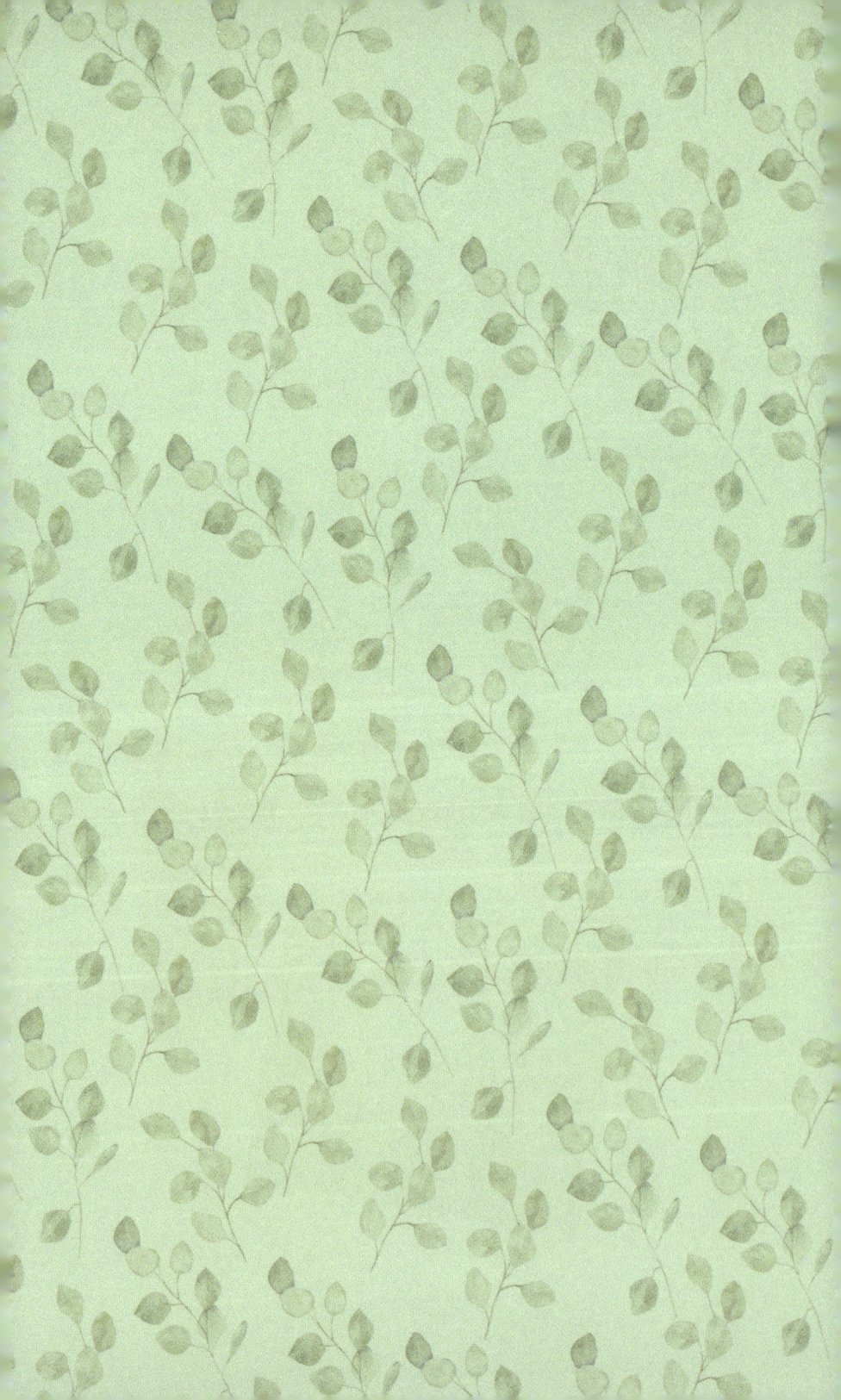

When I Was Born

*"A baby is God's opinion
that the world
must go on."*

Carl Sandberg

When I was born, my family lived in: _____

_____

_____

(Describe your home when you were a newborn.) _____

_____

_____

_____

_____

_____

_____

_____

_____

My earliest memory is... _____

_____

_____

_____

_____

_____

_____

·········· with **you** in mind ··············

The year I was born, the President of the United States was:

_____

_____

When I was a newborn baby, I slept in: _____

_____

_____

_____

I was baptized/dedicated: _____

(Give date and place.) _____

_____

_____

My God-parents/sponsors were: _____

_____

_____

```
BAPTISM
PHOTO
```

My very first playmate was: _____

_____

_____

Together we would... _____

_____

_____

_____

_____

_____

_____

PHOTO WITH AN
EARLY PLAYMATE

My Childhood

*Jesus loves
the little children,
all the children
of the world...*

My childhood home was: _____

_____

_____

_____

_____

_____

My favorite room in the house was: _____

_____

I liked it because... _____

_____

_____

_____

_____

_____

Our neighborhood was... _____

(Describe it.) _____

_____

_____

_____

_____

A toy that was special to me was: _____

_____

_____

_____

_____

_____

_____

_____

A homemade toy that I treasured was: _____

_____

(Who made it for you?) _____

_____

_____

_____

_____

_____

_____

_____

As a small child I struggled with... _____

_____

_____

_____

_____

As a child I excelled at... _____

_____

_____

_____

_____

_____

CHILDHOOD
PHOTO

The pets we had in our home were... _____

_____

_____

_____

_____

(What did your pets mean to you?) _____

_____

_____

_____

_____

_____

_____

When I was little I was afraid of... _____

_____

_____

My favorite candy was: _____

_____

_____

A book that I enjoyed having read to me was: _____

(Who read it to you?) _____

The friends I remember most
from my childhood are: _____

_____

_____

_____

_____

_____

My favorite hideout or clubhouse was:_____

_____

_____

(Describe it and your friends who joined you in that place.)

_____

_____

_____

_____

_____

As a child, my favorite meal was: _____

_____

A special family recipe
from my childhood: _____

_____

_____

_____

_____

_____

_____

_____

I started school when I was _____ years old.

I attended school at: _____

Transportation to school was by: _____

_____

_____

It was _____ blocks/miles from my house.

PHOTOS FROM
ELEMENTARY SCHOOL

My favorite elementary school teacher was:_____

(What did you appreciate most about that teacher?) _____

My favorite subject in school was: _____

I liked it because... _____

The subject at school I found
most challenging was: _____

_____

_____

_____

If I ever got into trouble in elementary school it was for...

_____

_____

_____

_____

_____

It isn't what we say that defines us,
it's what we do.

Jane Austen

An award or honor that I received in school was:

_____

_____

_____

A childhood hobby I was fond of: _____

It taught me... _____

_____

_____

_____

Lessons that I received outside of school were...

_____

_____

(Did you take music or dance lessons?) _____

_____

An outing that our family enjoyed was... _____

_____

(Describe where you went and what you did.) _____

_____

_____

_____

_____

As a child, my favorite sport was: _____

(Were you part of a team?) _____

_____

_____

My most memorable childhood birthday was... _____

_____

It was special because... _____

_____

I remember visiting my grandparents at: _____

_____

(Describe their home.) _____

_____

_____

The best thing about being with my grandparents was...

_____

_____

_____

_____

_____

_____

What I remember most about my grandparents is: _____

_____

_____

_____

_____

PHOTO WITH
GRANDPARENTS

"Train up a child in the way he should go,
and when he is old
he will not turn from it."
Proverbs 22:6

An important lesson I learned

from a grandparent was...

At home my chores included: _____

_____

_____

(Did you receive an allowance for doing chores?) _____

_____

_____

Doing regular chores taught me... _____

_____

_____

_____

_____

The church my family attended was: _____

_____

_____

_____

My most vivid memories of being in church are... _____

_____

_____

_____

_____

My favorite church songs were: _____

_____

_____

_____

_____

_____

On Sunday afternoons, my family and I would... _____

_____

_____

_____

_____

_____

_____

_____

_____

_____

_____

_____

_____

_____

_____

As a child, an adult who seemed
"larger than life" to me was: _____

_____

_____

(Describe that special person.) _____

_____

_____

_____

_____

_____

_____

_____

_____

_____

_____

As I Grew Up

"*School days, school days,*
dear old golden rule days...
reading and writing and 'rithmetic...
talk to the tune
of the hickory stick..."

Gus Edwards & Will Cobb

I attended middle school at: _____

I attended high school at: _____

Transportation to high school was by:

(Walking, biking, etc....) _____

_____

_____

_____

After school, my friends and I liked to... _____

_____

_____

_____

_____

_____

PHOTO WITH
HIGH SCHOOL
FRIENDS

If we ever got into mischief it was... _____

_____

_____

_____

A sport that interested me in high school was: _____

_____

_____

_____

_____

_____

_____

_____

_____

While I was in high school, my job was: _____

_____

_____

I was paid: _____

By working during high school I learned... _____

_____

_____

_____

This influenced my working life by... _____

_____

_____

As a teenager I volunteered for: _____

_____

_____

My favorite extracurricular activity was: _____

_____

_____

(What clubs, teams, or youth groups did you join?) _____

_____

_____

_____

_____

"There are far, far better things
ahead than we leave behind."
C. S. Lewis

A favorite vacation destination for our family was: _____

_____

_____

We enjoyed it because... _____

_____

_____

_____

PHOTOS FROM
A FAMILY VACATION

The funniest thing that happened to our family on a trip...

_____

_____

_____

_____

My best friend during high school or college was:_____

_____

_____

Together we... _____

_____

_____

_____

_____

PHOTO WITH
BEST FRIEND(S)

A valuable lesson I learned from my father was...

_____

_____

_____

_____

I am very grateful my mother taught me to...

_____

_____

_____

_____

A book that captured my attention during high school was:

_____

_____

It interested me because... _____

_____

_____

During high school I attended church at: _____

_____

_____

My faith in God was nurtured by... _____

_____

_____

_____

_____

_____

_____

_____

_____

"Faith is deliberate confidence
in the character of God whose ways
you may not understand at the time."
Oswald Chambers

A time that my faith was challenged... _____
(What got you through?) _____

_____

_____

_____

Family jokes or pranks
that kept us laughing for years... _____

_____

_____

_____

(Did anyone get in trouble over these?) _____

_____

_____

_____

_____

A fashion trend when I was in high school... _____
(How did this trend affect you?) _____

_____

_____

_____

_____

The person(s) who taught me to drive... _____

_____

_____

The first car I ever drove was a: _____

_____

_____

Our family car was a:_____

_____

_____

What were your feelings about that car? _____

_____

_____

Were you proud of it? _____

_____

_____

Did it embarrass you? _____

_____

_____

A special dance I attended during high school was:

_____

_____

Where was the dance held? _____

_____

_____

Who was your date? _____

_____

What kind of music did you dance to? _____

_____

Other things I remember about that night: _____

_____

_____

_____

_____

_____

_____

_____

_____

As I graduated from high school
my goals and aspirations were... _____

_____

_____

_____

_____

HIGH SCHOOL
GRADUATION
PHOTO

Further Education

"The great thing about
getting older
is that you don't lose
all the other ages
you've been."

Madeleine L'Engle

When I first left home I felt... _____

_____

_____

_____

I went to college, technical school,
or served in the military at: _____

_____

_____

_____

God blessed me with an aptitude for: _____

_____

This ability allowed me to... _____

_____

_____

The greatest thing I learned
during these years... _____

_____

_____

_____

_____

My best friends during college
or in the military were... _____

_____

_____

_____

Together we... _____

_____

_____

_____

Photos taken at college, technical school, or in the military.

_____

_____

_____

_____

My thoughts on the importance of higher education are...

_____

_____

_____

_____

_____

One event that completely changed
the direction of my life was..._____

_____

_____

A cause that I felt passionate about as a young adult...

_____

_____

(Did you participate in a rally
or a demonstration regarding this issue?) _____

_____

_____

_____

_____

_____

_____

A professor or mentor who encouraged me during my early twenties was: _____

_____

_____

This person influenced the way I thought about...

_____

_____

_____

_____

_____

_____

Honors I received in college or in the military: _____

_____

_____

_____

_____

_____

_____

_____

_____

_____

_____

During this time, my spiritual life grew... _____

_____

_____

_____

_____

_____

_____

My journey of faith was influenced by..._____

_____

_____

_____

_____

Were you aware of anyone who prayed for you regularly?

_____

_____

_____

Did you attend Bible Study? _____

_____

_____

_____

Love and Marriage

"To love another person

is to see

the face of God."

Victor Hugo from *Les Misérables*

The first time I realized someone had a crush on me...

_____

_____

(How did you feel about it?) _____

_____

My first date was with: _____

(Where did you go and with whom?) _____

_____

_____

My first boy/girlfriend was: This relationship taught me...

_____

_____

I met my spouse at: _____

_____

The qualities that first attracted me to him/her were... _____

_____

_____

_____

A fun date that still makes me smile... _____

_____

I knew he/she was the right one for me when... _____

_____

_____

"The secret of a happy marriage
is finding the right person.
You know they're right
if you love to be with them all the time."
Julia Child

A favorite pastime we enjoyed together was... _____

_____

_____

_____

_____

Our engagement became official on: _____

_____

(Describe the proposal.) _____

_____

_____

_____

_____

_____

WEDDING PHOTO

Our wedding date and time: _____

Our wedding took place at: _____

_____

(Describe the church or venue.) _____

_____

_____

Special highlights of our wedding day included...

_____

_____

(What did you wear? Who stood up for you? What songs and scripture readings were included in the ceremony? Did you have a special "first dance" song? What kind of wedding cake did you have?) _____

_____

_____

_____

_____

_____

_____

We honeymooned at: _____

(Where do you go? For how long?) _____

_____

_____

HONEYMOON
PHOTO

The most hilarious moment of our honeymoon was when...

_____

_____

_____

_____

_____

The greatest adventure we shared on our honeymoon was...

_____

_____

_____

_____

_____

Our first home was... _____

_____

(What do you remember most about that home?) _____

_____

_____

_____

The greatest adjustment to marriage was... _____

_____

_____

_____

As a newly married couple, some of our best friends were:

_____

_____

_____

_____

_____

Together we enjoyed... _____

_____

_____

_____

_____

As newlyweds, a favorite home-cooked meal was...
(Which of you did most of the cooking? Did that change through
the years?) _____

_____

_____

_____

The first church we joined together was: _____

_____

We chose it because... _____

_____

_____

As newlyweds we spent holidays...
(Where did you celebrate Thanksgiving and Christmas?)

_____

_____

_____

The most fulfilling aspect of our marriage has been...

_____

_____

_____

Our relationship was strengthened because of...

_____

_____

_____

_____

_____

_____

_____

What I appreciate most about my husband/wife now is...

_____

_____

_____

_____

_____

_____

_____

_____

_____

_____

_____

_____

If I could share one piece of wisdom
about marriage it would be...

_____

_____

_____

_____

_____

_____

_____

_____

_____

_____

_____

_____

Parenting

*"Life affords
no greater responsibility,
no greater privilege,
than the raising
of the next generation."*

C. Everett Koop

The news of our first pregnancy caused us to feel... _____

_____

_____

_____

When our first baby was on the way we lived at: _____

_____

_____

(Describe your circumstances at that time.) _____

_____

_____

_____

To prepare our home for a baby we... _____

_____

_____

_____

Visitors who came to meet our newborn... _____

_____

_____

_____

_____

Becoming a parent changed our life by... _____

_____

_____

_____

_____

(What were the practical day-to-day changes as you transitioned to parenthood?) _____

_____

_____

_____

_____

The greatest joy of parenting is... _____

_____

_____

_____

_____

_____

The hardest aspect of parenting is... _____

_____

_____

_____

_____

Becoming a parent caused my faith to... _____

_____

_____

(Describe how your prayer life changed when you became a

parent.) _____

_____

_____

When/if more children arrived, our home transitioned again.

_____

_____

_____

(Describe in what ways it changed.) _____

_____

_____

_____

PHOTO WITH
YOUNG CHILDREN.

A wonderfully vivid memory with our
babies/young children was when... _____

_____

_____

_____

_____

Activities that we most enjoyed with our little ones...

_____

_____

_____

_____

Our favorite family pets included...

_____

_____

_____

(Describe their place in the family.) _____

_____

_____

_____

_____

_____

When I became a parent my heart...

_____

_____

_____

_____

_____

_____

_____

"Sometimes," said Pooh,

"the smallest things take up

the most room in your heart."

A.A. Milne

A memorable vacation we took with our children was to...

_____

_____

_____

_____

The storybook our children requested the most was:

_____

_____

They liked it because... _____

_____

_____

The most important characteristic we nurtured in our children...

_____

_____

_____

_____

_____

If I could turn back the clock and do anything different
as a parent, it would be... _____

_____

_____

_____

_____

_____

_____

"Each day of our lives we make deposits
in the memory banks of our children."

Charles R. Swindoll

If my children and grandchildren have
learned anything from me I hope it is...

_____

_____

_____

_____

Becoming a parent taught me... _____

_____

_____

_____

Becoming a grandparent taught me... _____

_____

_____

_____

Work

"And whatever you do,
work at it with all your heart,
as working for the Lord,
not for men."

Colossians 3:23

My first job after high school was: _____

_____

_____

The most difficult aspect of this job was... _____

_____

_____

My first regular paying job was: _____

(Describe your responsibilities...) _____

_____

_____

_____

My first career-oriented job was: _____

This position taught me... _____

_____

_____

PHOTO TAKEN
ON THE JOB

During all of my working years,
the job that I enjoyed the most was... _____

_____

_____

_____

(Explain why you liked it and what you gained by doing it.)

_____

_____

The worst job I ever had was... _____

_____

_____

(In what ways was it the worst?) _____

_____

_____

The job-mentor or boss who gave me
the greatest encouragement: _____

_____

_____

(What did you learn from that person?) _____

_____

_____

_____

I found that if you love life; life will love you back.

Arthur Rubenstein

A job-related move that we made...

_____

_____

(Were you required to relocate for your work,

or was it a choice?) _____

_____

If I could start my career over I would... _____

_____

_____

_____

Special friendships that formed because of my work... _____

_____

_____

Work-related travel took me to: _____

_____

(How did you feel about traveling for work?) _____

_____

_____

Celebrations
and Milestones

*There is a time for everything
and a season for every
activity under heaven...
a time to weep and a time to laugh,
a time to mourn
and a time to dance...*

Ecclesiastes 3:1, 4

When I was a child our family celebrated birthdays by...

_____

_____

_____

A special birthday dinner or birthday cake

that I requested was... _____

_____

_____

_____

A birthday gift that meant a lot to me was: _____

_____

_____

_____

It was given to me by: _____

_____

_____

_____

A homemade gift that I made for a family member was...

_____

_____

(How did you create this gift?) _____

_____

_____

A BIRTHDAY
PHOTO

"Today you are you!
That is truer than true!
There is no one alive
who is you-er than you!"
Dr. Seuss

My fondest memory of a birthday celebration is...

_____

_____

_____

_____

When I became a parent, a birthday tradition

that we carried on was... _____

_____

_____

_____

_____

Our family celebrated Thanksgiving by... _____

_____

_____

A traditional Thanksgiving dish we ate was: _____

_____

_____

(How well did you like it?) _____

_____

_____

As a child, our family celebrated Christmas by... _____

_____

_____

_____

A traditional Christmas meal in my childhood home was...

_____

_____

_____

(How did you feel about eating it?) _____

_____

_____

A recipe for a family favorite Christmas Dish...

_____

_____

_____

_____

_____

_____

A Christmas pageant or program I participated in as a child...

_____

_____

_____

My fondest memory of that experience was...

_____

_____

_____

_____

"Christmas, my child, is love in action.
Every time we love, every time we give, it's Christmas."
Dale Evans

My favorite Christmas carols are: _____

_____

_____

_____

_____

_____

(Describe a time when you went Christmas caroling.)

_____

_____

_____

_____

As a parent, my most meaningful Christmas memory is:

_____

_____

_____

_____

_____

_____

My favorite holiday is: _____

_____

_____

I like it the best because... _____

_____

_____

_____

My favorite way to celebrate it is... _____

_____

_____

_____

On the Fourth of July our family would...

_____

_____

_____

As a child, another holiday that was particularly special
for my family was: _____

_____

We celebrated it by... _____

_____

_____

The most romantic Valentine
I ever received was... _____

_____

_____

_____

_____

_____

As an adult, my favorite
wedding anniversary celebration was...

_____

_____

_____

_____

_____

"Love is not weakness.

It is strong.

Only the sacrament of marriage can contain it."

Boris Pasternak

Becoming a grandparent
changed my life by... _____

_____

_____

_____

(Describe what it felt like to suddenly have a grandchild.)

_____

_____

_____

_____

To me grandchildren are... _____

_____

_____

_____

_____

_____

_____

_____

_____

_____

During My Lifetime...

"There are far, far
better things
ahead
than we leave
behind."

C.S. Lewis

The most joy-filled time of my life was... _____

_____

_____

_____

_____

The most exhausting time of my life was... _____

_____

_____

_____

_____

The greatest scientific advance made during my lifetime was...

_____

_____

It influenced the way I lived by... _____

_____

_____

_____

_____

_____

The most surprising "small world story" I ever
experienced was... _____

_____

(How was God working in this situation?) _____

_____

_____

The greatest difference between the world when I was ten years
old and the world now... _____

_____

_____

When I needed counsel or guidance most, I turned to:

_____

_____

_____

This was helpful because... _____

_____

_____

_____

_____

A personal accomplishment that still amazes me...

_____

_____

_____

The worst tragedy or sadness that happened to me

or to a loved one... _____

_____

_____

_____

_____

_____

(Does the memory of it seem different now

than when it first occurred?) _____

_____

_____

_____

_____

_____

A speaker or presentation that strongly influenced my life was:

_____

_____

(How were you impacted by this experience?) _____

_____

_____

My most valued possession is: _____

_____

_____

It means a lot to me because... _____

_____

_____

The most difficult choice I ever had to make was... _____

_____

_____

_____

If I had to make that decision again I would... _____

_____

_____

_____

The most exhilarating trip I ever took was:

_____

_____

_____

(Tell about your journey and what was special about it.)

_____

_____

_____

_____

_____

Coming home felt like... _____

_____

_____

TRAVEL
PHOTO

A time when I sensed God speaking directly to me was...

_____

_____

(How did this influence your life?)

_____

_____

_____

"There are two great days in a person's life—
the day we are born
and the day we discover why."
William Barclay

The people who have made
the biggest impact on my life are...

_____

_____

_____

_____

_____

_____

A person I have always admired is: _____

_____

I admire them because... _____

_____

_____

The hardest thing I've done in my life so far...

_____

_____

_____

_____

_____

_____

_____

Hopes and Dreams...

"Now faith is being sure of what we hope for and certain of what we do not see."

Hebrews 11:1

My greatest desire for my grandchildren is...

_____

_____

_____

When I was twenty-one, I wish I had known...

_____

_____

_____

The best encouragement
I could give my descendants is...

_____

_____

_____

_____

_____

A RECENT PHOTO
WITH GRANDCHILDREN

A book I hope everyone in my family will read is: _____

_____

_____

I feel this way because... _____

_____

_____

_____

The most important friendships of my life have been...

_____

_____

_____

These friendships have impacted my life by...

_____

_____

_____

My idea of success is...

_____

_____

_____

A time when I sensed God calling me to serve him was...

_____

_____

(What happened?) _____

_____

_____

Some goals I have for the next ten or fifteen years are...

_____

_____

_____

_____

_____

_____

Over the years my priorities have changed to include...

_____

_____

_____

_____

(How are your values different now than they were thirty years ago?) _____

_____

One thing I would not want to change about the way I have lived is: _____

_____

_____

_____

A hobby that gives me great pleasure today: New things I'm learning are: _____

_____

_____

_____

A valuable life lesson that I would like to share with my grand-children is... _____

_____

_____

_____

"Let the word of Christ dwell in you richly
as you teach and admonish one another with all wisdom,
and as you sing psalms, hymns and spiritual songs
with gratitude in your hearts to God."

Colossians 3:16

What I value most about our family is: _____

_____

_____

_____

_____

_____

_____

A portion of scripture that means a lot to me is: _____

_____

_____

_____

_____

_____

_____

It reminds me... _____

_____

_____

_____

_____

Every day my prayers for my family include... _____

_____

_____

_____

_____

_____

_____

additional notes

and photos

·· with you in mind ··

.... with you in mind ....

PHOTO

.... with you in mind ....

with you in mind

PHOTO

with you in mind

Published by KPT Publishing
Minneapolis, Minnesota 55406
www.KPTPublishing.com

ISBN 978-1-944833-20-6

Design: Abeler Design, Minneapolis, MN.

First printing March 2017

10 9 8 7 6 5 4 3 2 1

Printed in the United States of America